Conversation Tactics:

9 Keys

to Success

I0476147

Ideal Ways to

Express Yourself

Table of Contents

Key#1: Conversation Tactics and Their Benefits

"A single conversation with a wise person is better than ten years of study."

A conversation is a spontaneous and intentional communication between two or more people. Humans are social and coherently dependent on each other for communicative purposes. Since the beginning of time, humans have been using various ways to communicate with each other in their effort to survive.

A conversation is somehow a formal interaction among people and in this era of socialization, where the world has become a global village, it is necessary for people to have strong communication skills. They need those skills for professional and for personal growth as well as for effective communication. Strong communication skills are necessary for a person to keep up with the modern social needs and the way for a person to develop communication skills is the use of effective conversation tactics.

Effective conversation is an essential life skill, and like every aspect of human personality, conversation has some ethics and norms which are commonly known as tactics of conversation. Everyone wants to be popular and to be admired by others, and if a person has the skill to use these conversation tactics effectively, then that person will manage to be admired.

Human beings need to communicate with each other for various reasons such as sharing their views, ideas, feelings, and attitudes. If a person doesn't have these conversation skills, then that person may not succeed in making others get what is meant all the time. Without the effective use of conversation tactics, one may end up in misleading the listeners or the receivers of the content. Lack of conversation tactics proves that communication could function as a barrier between people. Effective communication is a skill that you can learn anytime in your life and learning conversation tactics will end up in polishing your personality and that could also be an asset in your professional life. It will be a tremendous investment that will give you many benefits that you are not able to get otherwise. With good conversation skills, all your communication will be fruitful to you and the people around you.

You can avoid personality drawbacks with the use of effective communicational tactics. What follows are some traits one must get rid of in order to have effective communication with others:

- Fear of people
- Shyness
- Low self-confidence

- Psychological issues to face people

The way a person speaks, namely that person's talking style and the way that person conducts a conversation have a great impact in the way that person present his personality to other people. Let us talk about some of the most significant benefits of the proper use of conversation tactics.

Benefits of Conversation Tactics

Conversation tactics benefit people in all paths of life. These skills are not only for professionals but are useful for all, regardless the position they hold in the society. A list of some benefits follows:

- Better Relationships

If you are able to use conversation tactics, which requires knowing how to talk with others then you are able to form better relationships. Formally, casually and professionally, you will be able to leave a positive image of yourself to others. People will try to talk to you as much as they can because they will enjoy talking to you. As a result, it will improve your relationships with others, and if you know how to behave and talk in any situation, then you know the key to success. Using conversation tactics, you can communicate with others in the most positive way. Especially when it comes to building your relations with your friends and family you must have good conversation skills so as to be able to express yourself properly.

Conversation mannerism can help you gain more acknowledgements in your professional life as well. For example, if you are a doctor and you are well versed and polite with your patients, you will inspire more trust to them than a doctor with a rude and emotionless talking style.

- Knowledge

Communication provides knowledge and that's a fact. Most of the facts and information you get comes from exchanging information with people when communicating. For instance, students always prefer those teachers who can impart their knowledge in a better way while communicating with them. A teacher with better conversation tactics manages to impart more knowledge to his or her students than a teacher who has the knowledge but is not able to communicate it. Just as, when we live our domestic life we learn and get all the information using conversation, either it is a babble form of an infant or an address from our parents. So we can say that all the information we get from our surroundings is because of this communication between us and our environment. Thus, the conversation can be a treasure of knowledge for us.

- A Positive Image

If one is capable of using good tactics of conversation, then that person will create a positive and everlasting image on others. Proper Communication enables one to get enough control on his or her emotions, and others will find that person appealing. Consequently, his or her personality will influence them forever. A positive image is the worthiest thing you will ever get when it comes to putting yourself out there.

- Peacefulness

As humans, we coexist with other people and it is only natural that there are some disagreements with other people that will have different views from time to time. If a person has good communication skills, then that person will be able to find a solution and converse without further trouble. If the solution to any disagreement comes through the medium of peaceful communication issues will be resolved in a very peaceful manner.

- Better Expression of Feelings

People have many ways to convey their feelings to others such as; through body language, gestures, behavior and most powerful among them is a conversation. Psychologists believe that one who can communicate well with others can have a higher level of admiration among others and can express his or her feelings in the most impressive way as compared to others who cannot use conversation tactics.

- Professional Achievement

Professional life is also as important as domestic life. Without knowing the ethics of good conversation, you can never achieve success in your professional life. Consider yourself in a professional scenario where you have to present a quotation for tender before the employees of another firm. If you are capable of communicating in a lucid manner, then your point will be clear to the other party, and it will increase your success chances.

Good communication is also what enables you to understand the jargons of different professions and it is your communication with others that determines your destiny in your professional career.

- Need to Globalize

Today being a global citizen is necessary. Distance is being reduced day by day and people are getting a chance to not only communicate nationally but internationally as well. So in this modern era, if you are good enough in conversation tactics, you will be able to give a good positive image for your nationality to other nationalities. Good conversation tactics that make positive impressions are able to bridge distance worldwide in a metaphorical sense of course.

- Psychological Dependence

As humans, we are psychologically dependent on each other for sharing our feelings and emotions as we can't remain isolated. We need counselling and suggestions regarding each and every matter, and this psychological dependence will be meaningless without the use of good conversation tactics

The conversation doesn't mean only speaking; it is a compiled form of body language, manners and verbal communication. It is not only a way to communicate or talk; it is a representation of one's personality and behavioral traits as well as the representation of one's manners and psychology.

Key#2: Psychological Analysis

Psychologists are of the opinion that an individual's personality traits can be manipulated during a conversation. Much literature has been documented in this psychological analysis, various psychologists have highlighted numerous facts. Following is a list of some of these interesting findings:

- If a person talks too swiftly, that person is considered very straightforward or blunt.

- If a person communicates in a soft and light manner, that person is thought to have calmness of mind.

- If one looks around during the conversation, that person is considered to have confusion in his mind.

- Looking down when in a conversation and talking with a low voice, shows shyness and indifference.

- Talking too much and babbling shows mental disturbance and character complexities.

Conversation and manners of discourse can be easily observed and detected through psychological analysis. In medical sciences, the conversation is a tool to diagnose psychological disorders as well as a method of cure. A large part of psychological counselling is based on a conversation with the patient. Politeness and conversation tactics can win a patient's trust and satisfaction which leads to healing of psychological disturbances and relieving stress and anxiety.

Conversation is more than just a way to speak; it is a cure as well. Medical research proves that adopting a polite and kind conduct with patients for one's conversation mannerism has a significant impact on the people around him. I would like to share a personal experience of mine in this regard. Once I paid a visit to my friend who was a student of applied psychology at a renowned university. She was doing her thesis on the impacts of discourse on the human mind. She surveyed at various hospitals and nursing homes. The results established that conversations play a pivotal role in calming people under various circumstances of critical nature.

During her research study, my friend met a woman at a subway station downtown. The woman appeared depressed and revealed to my friend that she would come to the subway station because she had no one to talk to, at home. During her half an hour conversation with the woman, my friend, discovered the lady was quite friendly and amicable and learned that drawing conclusions and making judgements without having a conversation with the concerned individual is wrong and misleading.

There are scores of researches and surveys that show the relationship between psychoanalysis and conversation. Everybody has a natural instinct to judge one's behaviour through the way a person talks in a particular situation. Thus, psychology and discourse are strongly correlated.

Psychology says that depression, anxiety, complexes and behavioural issues can be easily resolved through the medium of negotiation and words. Psychiatrists hold a person's hands to prevent him or her going deep into depression; and to stop the complications of mental disorders. Once I have read,

"The happiest conversation is that of which nothing is distinctly remembered, but a general effect of a pleasing impression.'

(Samuel Johnson)

This saying is quite meaningful as it argues that a good conversation always leaves a sense of pleasure in the minds of the participants. This impression heals the injuries of the soul, and it is a kind of therapy used in psychology in attempts to overcome mental disturbances.

In this age of hectic lifestyle, we all need some kind of conversation medication and therapy to reduce stress. Research shows that sharing your feelings and concerns with another person is the best way to reduce stress. In other words, a good conversation is a solution to all psychological needs.

Next, we will discuss the importance of personal charisma with regards to conversation tactics.

Key#3: Personal Charisma

"Words have magic and the way we articulate them, has magic too."

Conversation manners not only communicate personality traits but they also tend to reflect some other personal characteristics. Communication and conversation have a great significance in our lives, and the way of talking creates a lifetime impact on others. This impact compels others to listen and it is a key trait to one's personality as it leads to success and acknowledgement. This personality trait is called personal charisma. Charisma means magic; a spell which enforces others to ponder upon your communication and makes your conversation worth listening and appealing.

Personal charisma is the magic of one's personality and is that person's way of talking. Charisma is a constellation of complex and sophisticated social and interpersonal skills. This charisma allows influencing others at the deeper level of emotions and creates strong relations with concrete foundations. Charisma brings the following features to one's personality:

- Emotional Expression

People who have charisma in their personality, communicate and express their feelings more genuinely and impressively. This manner of their personality makes them affect others' moods and helps them be convincing on every matter. People use to trust this kind of people more compared to those who do not have a charismatic personality.

- Emotional Reliability

Personal charisma makes individuals more positive towards other people. Those individuals can respond to others' emotions in a healthier manner, and they can get more satisfaction and peace of mind. Other people rely on them for their emotional needs, and that gives them confidence and courage to do more for others and that's why we can see that good social worker are mostly good speakers.

- Self-control

Where personal charisma allows others to trust the charismatic individuals, it also gives these individuals, more control of their emotions. Personal charisma inculcates a balanced flow of emotions in charismatic personnel, making it possible to deny the importance of self-control in our day-to-day life.

- Healthier Relations

Personal charisma makes one able to have healthier relationships as compared to others who don't have a personal charisma and therefore are not able to understand others, and their points of views and also to pursue others on their own viewpoints. Having a personal charism is an extremely positive thing in a relationship since the understanding level is high then there will be a little chance of confrontation which allows for a social acquaintance to cherish.

We also need to keep in mind the type of conversation and to participate accordingly. We will discuss some of the major types of conversation in the next key, along with their main characteristics.

Key#4: Types of Conversation

Personal charisma is important for a successful conversation, but one must not forget to consider the scenario and the type of conversation in order to act accordingly. Conversation tactics is a vast topic to describe and are also categorized in kinds. Conversation tactics have a complete structure just like every profession and situation have its own conversation tactics. We will explain some of them below:

- Casual Conversation

Casual conversation refers to a conversation undertaken in a carefree manner. This kind of conversation is commonly used among friends and family members. While talking to the ones close to us, we don't have to be so careful about the discourse, and we don't have to be so conscious although we must respect the basic codes of conduct and ethics.

- Formal Conversation

Formal conversation is used in public gatherings and feasts when you have to meet so many people and keep the element of prestige and positive attitude in your conversation. In a formal conversation, we have to be conscious about your every word.

- Professional Conversation

Almost 90% people of us are professionals in any aspect of job or business and have to spend most of our time in professional life. Professional life has its own demands, and the most essential of those demands is the use of perfect professional language and jargons that are required in a profession. According to our professional needs, we have to develop our conversation tactics. For example, a doctor, has to use specific and polite conversation tactics, but a judge, should have element of strictness and discipline so as to keep the house in order and establish an esteemed image.

- Counselling

Counselling is also a conversation tactic. This kind of conversation is greatly admired and used by psychotherapists in an attempt to help people solve their minor problems with healthy and fruitful conversations. Counselling is the most effective type of conversation with the power to create huge impact.

- Speech or Passive Conversation

This type of conversation is mostly used in political or religious addresses. Speakers have to deliver what they want to say despite thinking that what they are saying has a spontaneous flow of emotions.

Moving towards the development of conversation tactics; the next key will concern the main tactics that help improve one's conversation ability that is expressed in the best possible manner.

Key#5: How to Develop Conversation Tactics

Once we know the primary types of conversation and their respective requirements, we can better use conversation tactics. These tactics are the rules that anyone can learn at any stage of their life. Some of these are explained in this section.

- Listening

It is an old saying that good listeners are always good speakers. Listening is the key to developing conversation tactics. Listening is somehow a wonderful way to inculcate best tactics of conversation in a sort of conversation setting where people are sharing their views and perspectives, and you are paying attention to what they are saying. That, subconsciously makes you a good speaker because you are paying attention to your surrounding and that helps you understand and respond accordingly. Good listening makes you focus on undivided focus, question and nods of agreements and disagreements that are essential for understanding and proper communication. Ultimately, these focal points will also sharpen your speaking skills.

- Knowledge of The Audience

In order to be a good speaker and to master your conversation skills, you must know your audience who you are talking to and what kind of language you have to use in that particular conversation. With professionals, you have to be careful to:

- Include Empathy

Empathy means accepting other people's viewpoints without feeling reluctant or resistant to others; respecting and granting everyone freedom of speech. When you are empathetic during your conversation and show convincing behavior towards others, you will be more attractive to others. Empathy and equality are basic conversation tactics that give you an opportunity to be popular.

- Having Positive Attitude

Having a positive attitude in conversations makes others trust you more. When you keep a more positive and friendlier attitude towards other people and show acceptance to their ideas and thoughts, people will be less hesitant towards you. There always some incidents in life when people come to you wanting to share their worries or asking for advice. A positive attitude A positive attitude gives you the courage to be more neutral in your attitude and behavior in such cases.

- Be Assertive

Assertive means to be more honest in defining what you need and what you want in a lucid manner.

Assertiveness is a key skill in your conversation tactics which makes your talk balanced and humble and people find you more genuine in your conversation which results in believing in you.

- Paying Attention to Audience's Body Language

People always show some kind of body language and gestures during a conversation, and this includes non-verbal signals and vibes. The human mind can interpret those signals and can understand most of other people's feelings during a conversation. So always try to pay attention towards what their body language shows and learn what people think during a conversation.

- Be Friendly and Humble

We notice in our daily life that people seem to be more attracted towards those who are more friendly and humble in their talking style. Friendly behavior makes you popular among you audience and makes other wanting to talk and share their views and problems with you as they feel comfortable while talking to you.

- Avoid Discrimination

This is the basic rule of conversation; non-discriminatory language should always be used during a conversation followed by a neutral body language. If you discriminate in your talking style, you will gradually lose your attraction and people will feel hesitated while talking to you.

- Be Responsive

Be responsive implies that you contribute to the conversation. Body language plays a vital role in the effectiveness of any conversation, and when you respond to your speakers, you show your presence and polishing your conversation tactics.

- Be informative

We usually notice in our daily life that some people seem very talkative and less beneficial than others. Always try to be beneficial to others and use the type of conversation that provides the other person with some kind of knowledge. In this way, people will respect you and listen to you.

- Be Logical

Without logic and reason, any kind of conversation and negotiation will end up in vain. Being logical and giving reasoning in a conversation makes your negotiation priceless and informative for others.

- Converse Smartly

Try not to use difficult vocabulary in a conversation. Be smart and impart ideas to others in a coherent manner. Be smart in your conversation to catch the maximum attention of your audience and people will respect and accept your ideas.

- Practice Emotional Intelligence

Emotional intelligence allows you to recognize and organize your emotions in conversations as most people try to focus more on appearances and expressions during a negotiation and to demean others. Emotional intelligence makes you aware of how to be more attractive without demeaning and how not to ignore others. It allows you to act wisely in situations where you have to be neutral and teaches you how to balance your emotions.

- Be Open-minded

Open mindedness is a worthy attribute of any conversation and makes you willing to walk away without any disturbance or confrontation if you have to face any opposition during negotiations. Open mindedness also makes you understand any possible opposition that can occur and helps you reach a conclusion.

- Be Patient and Calm

Patience and calmness of mind are essential in every aspect of a fruitful and peaceful conversation. Sometimes people openly oppose you or try to confront you, and if you do not keep calm the situation will worsen, and you will lose your audience. Rushing through such a situation or losing your temper may lead to worsening the situation and people losing their trust towards you. Also, if you have patience, you will be able to deal with anxiety and fear.

- **Think Before You Speak**

Your words determine what you are and where you stand in any situation and always ponder upon your words before articulating them otherwise you will have to pay for your words. Wise and useful words are always admired and praised by others, and if you speak without determining that either your words are consoling or hurting for the listeners, you will demolish your image.

- **Don't Be Reluctant or Confused**

Confusion and reluctance will minimize your chances to win audience's hearts. Strengthen your way of talking and be confident on what are you trying to say and stick to your purpose of conversation otherwise you will not be impressive to others.

In a professional environment, global and social conversation tactics are required to achieve the best results. The next Key focusses on them.

Key#6: Workplace, Global and Social Conversation Tactics

There are some norms of professional conversation that one must follow; some important tactics to become a better participant in a professional scenario in this modern global village. It is an old saying that humans are social beings and due to that we have a personal and a social need to communicate with each other. In all fields of our life, we have to communicate with others and not just with our family and friends but with our colleagues at work, with our fellows at travel. Thus, conversing is a basic need like food and air, without communication, we cannot survive this world. Nowadays, people are communicating all around the world without being conscious about their nationalities and set of beliefs.

Effective communication skills and worthy conversation tactics always strengthen your social circle. Effective communication skills make people love having you around and enjoy listening to you. Workplace conversation tactics are necessary; the office is not only a place where you spend time or go to earn money, but it is a grand social environment where you build relations with your co-workers, and you get to know your surroundings. It is really important for people to forge a positive image on others at their workplace. In any profession, your way of talking says a lot about you even if you are going to get a promotion or a bonus. Your progress at your workplace is 90% determined by your ethics in your conversation and the way you present yourself to others.

Researchers found that people who are better than others in their official conversations are more likely to be progressive in their profession. In this era of competition, people are more prone to get knowledge of conversation tactics. Suppose you are working in a company, and you have to deal with clients throughout the day, if you have good conversation tactics, clients will automatically be attracted to you, and this will increase the company's revenue. Good workplace tactics also allow you to convey your suggestions and share your views with your boss in an effective way and prove yourself to be a competent person.

Nowadays people at various workplaces, employees are specifically trained on how to deal with their clients. Employers try to make their employees good speakers and listeners. Many companies and business organizations are now making their social media sites and helplines where conversation tactics are essential to satisfy the customers or clients, and verbal communication is necessary to guide the customers. Most companies and individuals are now connected through social media applications like Facebook or WhatsApp which are easy and convenient to use. Professionals are making a difference in their workplaces because of their communication skills.

Thus, we can say that workplace tactics have a vital role in professional progress and growth in order to be good and effective professionals we have to learn those workplace conversation tactics.

Professional, conversation tactics are explained below in a more detailed way:

- Listening to Your Co-workers

Any type of conversation requires listening to others. Conversing and negotiating with others on professional matters requires good conversation skills. If you have good skills, you are better equipped to encourage people to adopt your viewpoints.

- Don't be Reluctant to Ask for Help

Nobody is perfect, and only time is required to gain skills relevant to any particular profession. Similarly, conversation tactics develop over time. You should always ask seniors for help and remember to keep the element of respect in your accent; this strategy develops a healthy relationship between you and your co-workers and ensures a friendly environment at your workplace.

- Be Appreciative To Your Colleagues

Appreciation plays a vital role in every profession. The strength of work can be doubled through encouragement and appreciation. Always adopt an attitude of appreciation towards your co-workers. Researchers said that some professionals, work for recognition and acknowledgement instead of money. Appreciative behavior towards your co-workers develops everlasting bonding among you and them.

- Be Responsive During Official Negotiations

Official meetings and negotiations always require more attention, and you must try to respond to your coworkers during meetings. Body language should be vigilant and attentive even in meetings. Lazy and less attentive body language plays a vital role in your career growth, as sometimes you can also feel like that you are not understanding a situation thoroughly but have to act the contrary.

- Utilize Quality Time in Conversations

Speedy conversations and talking in a quick manner can create confusion while conversing in brief and a quality conversation is always welcoming in professional environments. To be a logical speaker, you must take your time on thinking logically and briefly rather than spending time on long and haphazard conversations.

- Keep a Record of Happenings

As a professional, one must keep a record of important facts and files to cope up with professional life challenges. This attitude will also help you in setting your short term and long term goals. A record keeping strategy always keeps you connected with others in the sense that other people will always find assistance and guidance in you if they need to retrieve information.

- **Planned Conversations**

Professionals try to be clear and transparent in their conversations, and a way to do it is pre-plan conversations. For example, to organize your ideas and thoughts so as for the concept to be clear.

- **Be Welcoming Towards Others' Views**

It is in human nature that our thoughts and views always vary from person to person. You should always keep welcoming behavior towards other people's views. Try to take criticism positively and keep in mind that improvement is a never-ending process. Be positive towards others' opinions and evaluate the feedback wisely so as to make room for improvements. When you talk to your co-workers, remember to be responsive and not reactive or emotional.

- **Don't Be Over-reactive**

Sometimes there is silence in a conversation. Be comfortable with it and do not rush to talk like this will be considered over-reaction and your image will be tarnished. So be professional and keep your emotions in control during professional conversations.

- Remember Your Co-workers' Names

Try to address your co-workers with their names as this strategy will get you closer to them and create healthy friendships at your workplace.

- Give Compliments

Throwing compliments is a way to maintain relationships. But remember, words and facial expressions should match while giving compliments.

- Ask Open-ended Questions

Avoid close-ended questions because this will minimize the opportunity to talk and lower interest during a conversation. Ponder upon your pronunciation while asking a question and give your companions a chance to talk with you in an attempt to develop their interest in a conversation.

- Pay Attention

You must pay attention to what is being said. Your body language must be positive and reflect your interest in the ongoing conversation. Body language is pivotal in verbal communication. People read others' gestures and expressions during a conversation to judge the level of interest in the subject and commitment. An apparent disinterest in the conversation is read negatively and is considered a careless attitude in official negotiations and dealings.

- Try to Make Your Conversation Interesting

Even in professional life, people want to have interesting conversations rather than boring official meetings. So being a well-versed speaker means that one is able to make their conversations interesting and draw attention during business meetings of presentations. By doing this, you will find that your coworkers and your colleagues are responding in a more attentive and healthier way.

- Time Your Conversation

Timing is crucial; you should practice timing your conversations. Let others elaborate on their thoughts. It is important that you let others convey their message completely. Neither does anyone like to be interrupted in between nor can you understand the actual meaning of what you hear. If you can understand the actual viewpoint of others, you can explain your ideas better. Timing is, therefore, a vital conversation tactic for all kinds of negotiations and dealings.

- Keep Yourself Updated

It is important that you have information about the current situation, recent events, and important developments. You should be able to respond to any references possibly made during a conversation. Many people are habitual of bringing current affairs and latest developments in fields of common interest into the conversation just to make them more interesting. You should keep yourself updated so that your conversations are more interesting and informative. A quick scan of newspaper headlines with your morning latte should prove helpful.

Apart from the news, keep your calendar updated for birthdays, homecomings and other social events and happenings in your circles. Professional relationships develop better in a friendlier environment; it is important that you maintain a certain level of openness with your co-workers.

- Be Language Learned

Linguistic literacy is a significant conversation tactic in the globalized world of the twenty-first century. The growing interconnectedness of individuals from various countries, cultural and racial backgrounds has increased the importance of multilingualism. It is difficult for a person to manage his professional dealings if he as clients who cannot converse in his native language. As a global citizen, you should be versed in more than one languages to make conversations more convenient and productive. To overcome the language barriers, the United Nations made English into a compulsory second language for all the member nations. The measure has helped in reducing linguistic barriers to a certain extent, making English the global Lingua Franca; however, the role of linguistic literacy in the establishment of stronger professional relationships remains critical. A subjective factor is the pattern of human nature which shows that people tend to be more open to those foreign nationals who can converse with them in their own language instead of a second language like English.

In the twenty-first century, globalization is a reality and the need for every country to survive in this transformed system of the socio-economic and political environment, and so linguistic literacy is an important conversation tactic. You should be literate in at least two languages to manage your professional relationships and dealings well.

- Develop Acquaintance

It is quite difficult to persuade a stranger to agree with your viewpoint. One should always develop a certain level of acquaintance with others before trying to convince them of anything. Some people might be neutral to a discussion with a stranger but may not approve his endeavours to bring them round to his point of view; however, if they understand a little of his nature through some initial conversation, it is more likely that they will participate willingly in the exchange of ideas while one tries to persuade rather than being offended by it. It is a common observation that people tend to pay more attention to those who are acquainted with them; therefore, establishing a sense of knowingness is vital in persuasive conversations.

- Use Affirmative Language

Be clear in your meaning and try to be affirmative in your conversations. Speak less and prefer quality speaking and firm words rather than useless long talks. Avoid contradictory statements which will increase the chance of ambiguity. Speaking in a clear way will keep your intentions clear and meaningful.

- Ensure Credibility

Credibility is something you must inculcate in your conversations. It is the quality of being trustworthy. You must know what you are talking about, never refer to any case or scenario you are not fully aware of, while making reference always use authentic and acclaimed sources and last but not the least establish your expertise and knowledge in the subject under discussion. If people find one's expertise to be sound enough, they tend to trust them more.

Always define your need in a lucid manner before others and express your self in a credible manner.

- Create Urgency

It is in human nature that if something seems urgent people are more inclined towards it. Individuals who are versed in persuasive tactics of conversations make ideas and thoughts into scarce resources and enforce urgency for their acceptance. Just as launching a product in the market without appropriate marketing and advertising cannot win a broad customer base, simply proposing an idea or thought without reasoning it, validating and establishing a sense of urgency about its acceptance and implementation one can never persuade people to agree with him. Creating urgency is an important tactic in persuasive conversations, people who can make their opinions seem appropriate for time and trends are more persuasive than others.

- Be Specific

One thought branches out to many opinions but you must use reasoning, references and examples which are relevant to your opinion. Sharing instances and impact of a certain idea on others is one of the most common persuasive techniques, but you must make it a point that the stories you tell are not irrelevant to the context of the whole discussion. Be very specific about your ideas and thoughts and advocate them concisely. If you step off the track it is quite probable that you may not be able to bring the discussion back to its original frame. While you should always be informative in your conversations, it is very important to be specific about the ideas you want to inculcate. An advocate can certainly never win a case if he speaks of an event which doesn't circumference his evidence and the line of argument. Relevance and specification are significant in persuasion.

- Be Comprehendible

Never speak too swiftly or too slowly during a conversation in general and a persuasive conversation in particular. Speak firmly and coherently. If people cannot hear every single word that you speak and ponder upon it, it is difficult for them to understand the message that is being conveyed to them. One must be audible and comprehendible in their speech to have a good convincing power. People who speak very fast generally tend to fail in persuading people to accept their viewpoint because the listeners cannot hear them clearly or interpret their words properly. You should always be fluent and firm if you want your words to have persuading power.

Contrary to speaking too fast, if you speak too slowly people tend to get bored, negligent and diverted. If one takes too long to present their points of views and validate them, listeners might just lose the string itself. You cannot persuade a person who stopped paying attention in the middle of the conversation and that is why you should always speak firmly and coherently, fluently yet understandably.

- Talk About the Incentives

The cost-benefit analysis is done before making a choice, whether it is about investing a sum of money or it is about accepting an idea. People tend to weigh the pros and cons and costs and benefits of the new propositions. In order to persuade people to agree with your opinion, you must give them an incentive. By incentives, in general discussions, the social and financial benefits are meant. It is human nature that people always seek a return for acceptance, whether it is an offer being accepted or simply a thought.

Unless you bait the fish you cannot catch; similarly, unless you give incentives you cannot bring people round to your viewpoints.

- Body Language

Your body language, gestures, postures and facial expression play a significant role in persuading people to accept your opinions. If you seem confident and aware of what you speak about, dedicated and inclined towards the idea you compel people to pay more attention to your validations and reconsider their own opinions simply because they can read your strong belief in your thoughts. Your self-confidence can persuade people. Show interest in the conversation, if others can see that you are willingly presenting your views and would like them to learn about them they listen more attentively and give a good thought to whatever they listen to. Also, people tend to be more open to others' opinions if they feel that others are welcoming to their ideas. It is, therefore, important that you must have a positive body language in order to persuade others.

Last, the choice of words is quite vital in conversations, you must choose your words wisely. Whether it is a persuasive conversation or a general discussion, it is important that you consider your words before you speak. Offending someone during a conversation or using inappropriate words can affect your communication negatively. The next Key discusses this important conversation tactic in detail.

Key#7: Body Language

Body language is a significant component of verbal communication, and its importance has grown over time with the rapidly growing process of globalization. Globalization has its impacts on society, and cultural practices and communication is not an exception. As interactions between people from various origins and native languages take place, body language is pivotal for meaningful exchanges. Since there exist linguistic barriers, people judge the intent and commitment by observing the body language, the responsive gestures, facial expressions, and movements. Gestures and nonverbal cues play a significant role during negotiations, and an individual with good communication skills can read gestures even if he cannot understand the language.

Body language is a core conversation tactic, and it is not only used by humans but animals as well. Body posture, eye movements, and facial expressions coherently express the emotions and sentiments of the conversant. Sign language is a form of body language which is used to convey messages by those who cannot speak; this fact highlights the significant impact that body language has on our conversations. Gestures and movements are more powerful tools of expressing thoughts and ideas as compared to speech at times. A human can naturally interpret other humans' body movements, and facial expressions and a person with sound communication skills can easily read others' thoughts on a matter simply observing their body language during a conversation. It is convenient to observe if one is interested in the conversation, uninterested or irritated by the exchange.

Interpretation of gestures and body movements varies greatly from country to country or from situation to situation, for instance; a thumbs up can be taken as a good luck wish or a signal towards the top. Interpretation of body language is subjective though.

Understanding and interpretation of body language are a vital skill in many professions such as applied psychology and criminal investigation. Communication is a key human practice and body language greatly impacts people's conversations. The study and systematic knowledge of body language are formally known as kinetics. Kinetics was first introduced by the American Anthropologist, Ray Birdwhistell. In the modern globalized world of today, the knowledge of kinetics is very important. Kinetics is a wide knowledge, and some of its most important parts are:

- Emblems

Emblems are the easily interpretable signals coming from the use of body language. They are comprehensible and can be directly translated into a sentence or a phrase. Emblems are the most easily recognizable form of gestures and body language. For example, the sign "V" with the help of hand and fingers can be easily interpreted as a victory. Same as the sign "O" is interpreted as good or okay. These are the easily interpretable signs we use to express our feelings in our daily lives.

- Illustrators

Illustrators are those signals of body language which reinforce the non-verbal signals to be translated in a verbal form and can be ambiguous and vary from place or situation. For example, pointing at someone or something the conversation is about. Illustrators are reinforcing signals. The use of illustrators is a common practice in Anglo-Saxon cultures which have no refined code of conduct, but in Asian cultures, use of illustrators is considered as a lack of intelligence.

- Regulators

Nonverbal signals which are used to regulate, moderate and keep the flow of a conversation are known as regulators in kinetics. They are often used to give feedback if the viewpoint of others has been clearly understood. For example, in some civilizations people use to nod their head and produce the sound of 'uh' 'uhhu' to show their understanding, in some other countries people use silence to express understanding. In our daily life, we use a lot of examples in conversations, and when a person wants to interrupt, that person raises their hand so as to indicate his/her need to interrupt or to say something.

In response usually, a nod is used to grant permission to the other person to speak and share their thoughts. The gesture as a tool to regulate the flow of the conversation and passing on the opportunity to speak to the other side without actually making an intervention that would break the flow.

- Adaptors

Adaptor shows the postural changes and other physical movements during conversations as the posture tells much about the interest or lack of understanding. If you see a person sitting in a fatigued or uncomfortable manner that person is showing a lack of interest. If a person sits in a vigilant manner, it shows the interest and understanding of the conversation. Adaptors are easy to understand and important part of kinetics that helps to polish your conversation tactics.

- Affect Displays

An action or affect display is the ultimate part of kinetics as it directly shows emotions. Some researchers say that the leg movement defines true feelings. We often see some people moving their legs while talking and this shows their understanding or their level of interest. Similarly, open and relax body posture shows the confidence. Thus, we can say that posture shows the moods, status, approval, warmth and other emotions.

All these types of body language define the complete knowledge of body language. Body language is essential in conversation tactics. We always use some kind of body language during our conversations as without this attribute our conversations can be as monotonous or boring as robots.

The conversation has a major objective, which is persuasion. In the next key, we are going to have a look at the ways we can persuade the listener.

Key#8: How to Persuade the Audience?

Body language performs one major function which is to persuade others by complimenting words. If body language does not complement words, people would not believe anything that is being said. It is important to persuade listeners. Being persuasive means to convince people to accept your viewpoints. Persuasive conversations are the most interesting kind of conversations as they involve proposition and opposition of ideas where good conversation skills tend to win. Disagreements can occur at any point during a conversation and may lead to a sudden loss of confidence. It is, thus, important to develop persuasiveness.

If you are persuasive in your conversations, you can inspire trust to others very quickly. It is a tactic used by every good speaker. Persuasiveness is by no means a trick; it is a conversation tactic. It is a compound of voice quality, postures, and gestures, vocabulary and jargons, etc. It is not about winning the discussion all the time; it refers to your reactions to a disagreement. You must keep your emotions under control and reason your statements before presenting your viewpoint to others. Also, an over-reaction to disagreements reduces the likelihood of cooperation. Your reactions must be balanced, and so, you must be persuasive in your conversations not assertive or naïve.

If you want to develop the persuasive conversation tactic, you must be very polite and rational in your behavior with others during a conversation. Always choose a strong way of talking and use examples to make others agree, logically. Try to present your views and ideas positively so that the listener does not take it as a personal offence. People are free to speak and express themselves in any way they wish and that is a fundamental human right. Whenever you start an argument in a conversation which you want to consider the fact that other people will have different opinions and if you want to persuade them in listening to yours then you should be sensitive towards their emotions and their opinions and consider their feelings. It is not easy to make others agree with you and if you want to persuade them then you must have in mind the rule below:

- Timing is Everything

It is not only your words and body language that persuade others but the timing of your statements as well; knowing the right time to talk and having the awareness and knowledge of how to talk so to get best results. If you want to make people agree with your point of view, you must approach them, when they are most relaxed and open to talk. I have learned through my personal experiences that people tend to be more easily persuaded when they are obliged. It is a general observation that people tend to be more welcoming to conversations and different viewpoints if they are complemented, thanked or humbled.

Key#9: Don't Get Stuck with Words

We talked about persuasion in the previous key but remember not to get yourself in a confusing situation when you are searching for a convincing diction during a conversation. Sometimes it happens that you can get stuck with words. That could be a bit embarrassing. It is quite common to get confused when selecting words while you are trying to propose a point of view, persuade someone or simply interact with a person. Such a confusion, like getting stuck with words can interrupt the flow of a conversation, break it and create inconsistency. Inconsistent conversations are less likely to be interesting and effective. A smoother flow of words, channelling of thoughts and expression of emotions is always appreciated. Fluent and continuous conversations tend to be more compelling and meaningful since the conversers pay more attention to what is being said.

Being able to continue a discussion without confusion and getting stuck with words is a vital conversation tactic specifically during presentations, proposals and negotiations. You must be able to address the queries effectively and without breaking the flow of the conversation. In order to improve consistency and flow of your communication, you should practice the following conversation tactics:

- Preparation

Prepare for the conversation you are going to have, a presentation, a business meeting or any other important discussion. You should know your argument, have knowledge of the basic concepts upon which you are basing your proposal, have a sound reasoning to validate your opinions and ideas and have logical answers to any possible queries, cross questioning and counter argument. If you are well-prepared for a conversation you have clarity in your head and a clearer mind means a clear and more concrete elaboration. You can speak better, be more eloquent and fluent if you already know what you wish to say. Selection of words is much easier if you have an answered prepared in your mind as compared to a spontaneous response to any query or critique.

- Attentiveness

It is important to remain attentive during a conversation. It isn't queer to have a hundred thoughts popping up in your head during a discussion, ideas and reminiscences can stem from any reference, scenario or a feeling that a converser or you yourself may speak of. You must not dwell on the past or get distracted from planning something for the future while a conversation is underway. Unorganized, racing random thoughts break your concentration and make things unclear, you cannot formulate your answers under this confusion and the flow is thus disrupted as you speak in puzzle while searching for verbal fillers. Stay attentive and remain in the present so that you may listen to everything that is being said, ponder upon and respond firmly, without confusion or getting lost for words. Concentration is important for almost everything that you do and so effective conversations require concentration and staying in the present during an interaction.

- One Topic at One Time Only

Complete one topic before moving on to a new on during your discussions. If you, introduce two more topics and discuss them simultaneously, you would get confused, there would be a cobweb of thoughts and opinions in your head you would not be able to organize your thoughts to formulate an answer which would result in disruption of the conversation's flow due to difficulty in selection of words. If you completely close a topic before starting a new one you keep your thoughts in an organized stalk instead of jumbling up and consequently your brain's processing of vocabulary improves as well. Multitasking decreases human brain's power to process thoughts, the same is true for simultaneous discussion over various subject. To avoid getting stuck with words you should make it a point to concentrate your thoughts on one particular topic at one time.

- Listening

Develop a habit of listening to others. A conversation is an exchange between two people, one must learn to listen to others rather than just being listened to. Let others speak, listen to them carefully, stay attentive and contemplate on what you hear. If you listen to other people you will pick words, terminologies and jargons which you can use in your statements. It is common to know some words but not being able to retrieve them from your brain, if you listen carefully to others you might pick the words from you vocabulary which may help you convey your message more effectively and fluently.

- Concision

You should be concise in your statements, convey your message completely and coherently but do not unnecessarily long explanations. You can express your opinions and thoughts by choosing the right words, you do not need to give lengthy explanations if you have use appropriate words. Many people tend to have this habit of repeating one thing multiple times in several sentences which are literally synonymous because they think that a longer explanation is more convincing. A more appropriate instead of a lengthier explanation is needed to be more persuasive during a conversation for you can use more powerful and appropriate words in a concise statement as compared to a deliberately dragged one. If you speak concisely, you won't get stuck for words and speak more fluently and effectively.

- Honesty

Honesty is certainly the best policy. You should be honest about your opinions, thoughts, ideas and contemplations in a conversation. If you speak the truth, you speak in a natural flow and the words come smoothly. On the contrary, if you fabricate and tell made-up stories your brain must process the content you are to speak. Deliberating an answer takes time in processing, you must search for the most appropriate words in your vocabulary for you are manipulating the facts. If you speak the truth, you know what the reality is and you simply speak of it in a descriptive manner instead of a manipulative and deliberate manner which is the case if you conceal your true opinions and emotions and tell a lie. If you have nothing to say, confess it so that the conversation can move on. There is no use of keep contemplating when your instinct is not responsive. Honest responses save you from confusion and getting confused for words.

- Keep Calm

No matter how critical or difficult a conversation is, one must always keep his nerves. You must realize that the more you get worked up and anxious about a conversation the more confusing it gets. If you feel nervous or anxious about a conversation, you will always be stuck for words. Confidence is the key, you need to be clear in your head and confident about your ideas and views. If you feel intimidated by anyone, just take a deep breath before you begin. If you feel anxious about anything, your mind gets confused and its processing power decreases which results in disruption of word flow. To keep the conversation fluent, it is important to have a clear and focused mind, and for that, you must keep your nerves and stay confident during a conversation no matter how difficult it is.

- Think

You must keep the thought process flowing during a conversation to render your brain some convenience in staying vigilant about the kind of vocabulary you must use during a conversation. Staying focussed during a conversation not only channels more relevant and better thoughts relevant to the subject of discussion but helps the words flow going as well. Keeping the thoughts organized and keep thinking during an interaction are one of the most important conversation tactics for several vital reasons and a smooth word flow is one of them.

- Curiosity

Curiosity keeps you completely engaged during a conversation, develop interest in the ongoing conversation to inspire inquisitiveness and curiosity which help the thought process to stay specific to the topic. If you are curious about a topic, you will have queries and that helps you think faster and better about a subject of discussion and so curiosity and inquisitiveness help the brain channel a smoother word flow during a conversation.

- Language Proficiency

If you are proficient in a language only then should you choose it as your medium of communication for any kind of communication, personal or professional. The world is now a global village and the probability of having a conversation with an individual from a different geographical, racial and linguistic background is much greater now. In order to keep the conversation flowing without any sort of disorder and a smooth word flow it is important that conversations are done in a language of one's proficiency. It is common that people can read and write in a particular language quite efficiently but their spoken skills are weak. You must work on your spoken language skills before you use it in a conversation. Read write literacy in language differs greatly from spoken proficiency, this difference is commonly ignored by people but it matters for a smoother word flow and effective conversing. Do not use a language for official dealings and negotiations or crucial personal discussions until you have enough knowledge of the language. Linguistic literacy is very important not only for persuasiveness in a conversation but for an uninterrupted word flow as well.

- Nobody's Perfect

Always remember that nobody's perfect and it is perfectly alright to pronounce a word wrongly or make a linguistic error once in a blue moon. You should not feel inferior or be too concerned about a perfect reasoning during your conversations. Inferiority complex and overthinking about a discussion would not help you in any way, rather it will confuse you and diminish your concentration as well as thinking capacity during a conversation. It is imperative that you must think clearly and confidently for a more productive conversation and an evener word flow. You will sound better if you are confident about what you say rather than being too confused in your consciousness and anxiety of not being good or being inferior to anyone. You don't have to be perfect, you only need to convey your thoughts in the most convincing manner and for that, it is important that you do not get stuck for words.

Keeping the thought process organized, developing an interest in the conversation, being inquisitiveness and maintaining a continuous flow of ideas along with being calm, confident and honest are some of the most significant conversation tactics to maintain a smooth and uninterrupted flow of words, your choice of words is clearer if you can think clearly about a certain subject and have adequate knowledge of the language of discussion.

Conclusion

Communication is one of the most important human activities for one's survival in this world, it is a need in our daily lives. Conversation skills are required to maintain healthy relationships, personal as well as professional. Developing better communication skills is one of the most significant components of personality building and for this reason, many organizations have introduced communication skills courses in on-the-job training over the past few years. Effective communication requires certain tactics and techniques to be employed. It is important that one talks clearly and coherently with logic, reasoning, and confidence. Persuasiveness is an important skill in conversations where in order to convince people to accept their ideas and views, one must present his case in a coherent and refined manner, an uninterrupted word flow certainly improves the effectiveness and persuasiveness of a conversation. This book highlights some of the most vital conversation tactics that must be worked on so as to refine one's conversation skills and improve the effectiveness of his or her communication with others.

www.ingramcontent.com/pod-product-compliance
Lightning Source LLC
Chambersburg PA
CBHW071818170526
45167CB00003B/1358